The Ultimate Canapé Collection

Celebrate in Style with an Elegant Selection of 40 Savory, Sweet, Canapé Cocktail Recipes

Table of Contents

INTRODUCTION 4

Savory 7

    Beetroot and Goat Cheese Crostini 8

    Cheddar Cheese and Red Onion Straws 10

    Coconut Seafood Salad 13

    Coronation Turkey Cups 16

    Cranberry and Brie Canapés 18

    Creamy Chicken Vol-au-Vents 20

    Creamy Hot Pastrami Filled Yorkies 23

    Grilled Zucchini with Peanut Chicken 25

    Mini Lamb Kebabs with Yogurt Sauce 28

    Mini Parma Ham Vegetable Tarts 31

    Moroccan Chickpea Patties 33

    Pecan-Stuffed Dates 36

    Polenta and Prosciutto Chips 39

    Ravioli Pops 41

    Salmon Mousse Canapés 44

    Spanish Skewers with Homemade Dip 47

    Spicy Salmon and Guacamole Cones 50

    Steak on a Stick 53

    Stilton and Chutney Rarebit Nibbles 55

    Sweet Corn Beignets with Spicy Salsa 58

Sweet 62

   Apple Pie Pastry Wedges 63

   Baby Caramel Rolls 65

   Caramel Cream Chocolate and Hazelnut Popsicles 67

   Key Lime Pie Shots 69

   Lemon Meringue Pots 71

   Mini Orange Cupcakes 74

   Mini Pastel Macarons 77

   Shortcakelettes 80

   Strawberry Cheesecake Pots 82

   Sweet Potato Cheesecakes 84

Cocktails 87

   Blood Orange and Lemon Prosecco Slushies 88

   Blueberry Lavender Fizz 90

   Brandy and Pineapple Party Punch 92

   Perfect Pimms 94

   Pink Lemonade 96

   Pomegranate Bellini 98

   Sgroppino 100

   Sparkling Royal Punch 102

   Strawberry and Watermelon Mojitos 104

   The Bee's Knees 107

INTRODUCTION

With buffets seeming to be a thing of the past and sit-down meals proving too much hassle, canapés are quickly becoming the new kid on the block.

The French were the first to offer canapés to guests as far back as the 18th century with Britain jumping on the canapé bandwagon at the end of the following century.

Today, canapés or as we often call them in modern times amuse-bouche, are a popular choice for lots of different social occasions.

But before you discover The Ultimate Canapé Collection of recipes, read on and find out just how your favorite finger foods have changed over the decades.

- If you were attending a party in 1953, you would definitely see Devilled Eggs take pride of place on the party spread
- The Swinging Sixties didn't just give us the Beatles, they also gave us cheese straws and salty crackers piped with cream cheese
- Remember the seventies? If you do, then you will recall tucking into cheese and pineapple sticks
- What was the considered the classiest canapé in the 1980s? Well creamy mushroom and chicken Vol au Vents of course!
- Fast forward to the nineties and expect to tuck-into smoked salmon canapés washed down by a chilled glass of champagne
- Warm asparagus with mozzarella cheese and sun-blush tomatoes were just one of the collection of canapés served at Prince Harry and Meghan Markle's 2018 royal wedding

A party finger food, canapés can be enjoyed while you stand, mingle, and chat.

From Steak on a Stick to Sweet Potato Cheesecakes, and more, The Canapé Collection will help you create all the recipes you will ever need for the perfect party.

Savory

Beetroot and Goat Cheese Crostini

An elegant and colorful canapé is a welcome addition to any dinner party or buffet table.

Servings: 20

Total Time: 20mins

Ingredients:

- 2 small frozen French baguettes
- Olive oil
- 7 ounces soft goat cheese
- 7 ounces sweet beetroot (cooked)

- Orange zest (to serve)
- Fresh thyme (to serve)

Directions:

1. According to the package directions, cook the frozen baguettes. Set aside to cool.

2. Slice each baguette into 10 equal portions.

3. Drizzle the slices of baguette with a drop of olive oil and place in the oven until crisp, for 5-6 minutes.

4. Spread the goat cheese over the toasted bread and top with the cooked beetroot. Slice into chunks and serve with a scattering of orange zest and a sprinkling of fresh thyme.

Cheddar Cheese and Red Onion Straws

Those Brits know a thing or two about cheese straws! And these crisp golden straws served with a homemade red onion dip will have everyone's mouth, watering.

Servings: 25

Total Time: 40mins

Ingredients:

- 1 (13 ounce) package ready-rolled puff pastry
- 4 tbsp store-bought red onion relish

- 4 ounces strong Cheddar cheese (grated)
- ½ medium-size egg (beaten)
- 1 tbsp sesame seeds

Dip:

- 1 small-size red onion (peeled, coarsely chopped)
- ¾ ounces flat-leaf parsley (chopped)
- 1-2 tsp small capers
- 2 tbsp extra-virgin olive oil

Directions:

1. Preheat the main oven to 425 degrees F. Line 2 baking trays.

2. Roll the pastry out into a 15" square.

3. Spread the red onion relish over half of the square, allowing a narrow border.

4. Sprinkle the grated Cheddar over the relish.

5. Fold the remaining half of the pastry over the top and press down gently to seal.

6. Brush the beaten egg over the pastry, before sprinkling with sesame seeds.

7. Cut the pastry into strips approximately ½" wide by 7½" long. Twist the strips and arrange them in a single layer on the prepared baking tray.

8. Bake in the oven until crispy and golden, for 12-15 minutes. Set aside on a wire baking rack to cool.

9. To prepare the dip: Add the red onion, parsley, capers, and oil to a jug, and using a blender, combine.

10. Serve the cheese straws with the dip.

Coconut Seafood Salad

Serve these creamy coconut and fish salad in small glasses and enjoy as a seafood canapé at your next party.

Servings: 6

Total Time: 20mins

Ingredients:

- ½ cup coconut milk
- 4 slices of fresh ginger

- 1 red chili (finely chopped)
- 1 tsp lemon zest
- ½ cup plain Greek yogurt
- Salt and black pepper
- 7 ounces cooked fresh white fish, of choice (cubed)
- 7 ounces cooked prawns (tails removed)
- Freshly squeezed juice of 2 limes
- 1 cup Cos lettuce leaves
- Mint leaves (to serve)
- Chili (chopped, and to serve)
- 1 fresh lime (sliced, to garnish)

Directions:

1. In a small pan, combine the coconut milk with the ginger, chili and lemon zest. Bring to simmer, and simmer for between 3-4 minutes. Remove the pan from the heat and set aside to cool before removing and discarding the slices of ginger.

2. Fold the Greek yogurt into the coconut milk mixture — season to taste with salt and pepper and stir gently to combine.

3. Fold the fish, prawns, and lime juice into the yogurt mixture.

4. Add the lettuce to the base of 6 small glasses.

5. Spoon the fish-yogurt mixture over the lettuce, garnish with mint leaves, chopped chili and a slice of fresh lime.

6. Enjoy.

Coronation Turkey Cups

No time to cook? No problem! These tasty Coronation turkey cups come together in no time at all.

Servings: 12

Total Time: 15mins

Ingredients:

- ½ -¾ cup plain yogurt (as needed)
- 2 tbsp full-fat mayonnaise
- 1 tbsp mango chutney
- 2 tsp mild curry powder
- Freshly squeezed zest and juice of ½ lemon

- 12 ounces leftover, cooked turkey (shredded)
- 1 small mango (diced)
- Handful of coriander (chopped)
- 3 Baby Gem lettuce leaves (torn)
- Toasted almond flakes

Directions:

1. In a bowl, combine the yogurt (as needed) with the mayonnaise, mango chutney, curry powder, lemon zest, and lemon juice. Taste and season.

2. Add the shredded turkey followed by the mango and coriander and mix to combine entirely.

3. Arrange the torn lettuce on a platter, spoon the turkey mixture over the top and garnish with toasted almond flakes.

Cranberry and Brie Canapés

Move over Cheddar cheese and pineapple; Brie and cranberry are the new best combination in town!

Servings: 12

Total Time: 25mins

Ingredients:

- 1 (6") French baguette
- Olive oil (to drizzle)
- ½ cup whole cranberry sauce
- 1 tsp rosemary (chopped)

- 1 tbsp premium balsamic vinegar
- 1 pound French Brie cheese

Directions:

1. Preheat the main oven to 400 degrees F.

2. Slice the baguette into ½" slices and arrange in a single layer on a baking sheet lined with parchment paper.

3. Drizzle the oil over the bread.

4. Transfer to the oven for 5-8 minutes, until lightly golden.

5. Take the baking sheet out of the oven.

6. In a bowl, combine the cranberry sauce with the rosemary and vinegar.

7. Cut the Brie cheese into pieces, slightly smaller than the bread.

8. Spoon the cranberry sauce on top of the toasts.

9. Arrange the Brie on top of the sauce, and grill on high for a couple of minutes, until the cheese melts.

10. Drizzle with balsamic vinegar and enjoy.

Creamy Chicken Vol-au-Vents

So, dishes stand the test of time, and these melt in the mouth Vol au Vents are proof positive that some oldies are golden!

Servings: 6

Total Time: 50mins

Ingredients

- 1 (17 ounce) package frozen puff pastry (thawed)
- 1 large-size egg

- 1 tbsp water
- 6 bacon slices
- 2 medium leeks (whites only, and sliced)
- 1 medium-size sweet yellow pepper (seeded, and diced)
- 1 cup cooked rotisserie chicken (shredded)
- 8 ounces cream cheese (softened)
- ¼ tsp salt
- ¼ tsp black pepper
- Fresh parsley (minced)

Directions:

1. Preheat the main oven for 400 degrees F.

2. On a clean and lightly-floured worktop, unfold one sheet of pastry. Using a 3¼" circular pastry cutter, cut 6 circles.

3. Arrange the pastry circles on a baking sheet lined with parchment paper.

4. Unfold the remaining sheet of pastry and cut 6 more circles. Using a 2½" pastry cutter, cut the middles out of the 6 circles to form 6 rings. Arrange each ring on top of one of the pastry circle on the baking sheet.

5. In a bowl, whisk the egg along with the water, and lightly brush it over the pastries. Chill in the fridge for 15 minutes.

6. Remove the pastry circles from the fridge and bake in the preheated oven for 20-25 minutes, until golden. Set aside to cool on a wire baking rack.

7. In the meantime, in a large frying pan, over moderate heat, crisp the bacon. Remove the bacon to kitchen paper towel to drain. Discard all but 1 tbsp of the bacon drippings.

8. Add the leeks along with the yellow pepper to the bacon drippings in the pan and over moderate to high heat, cook for 5-7 minutes, until fork tender.

9. Turn the heat down to low, stir in the bacon along with the chicken, cream cheese, salt and black pepper. Cook, while stirring until entirely blended before removing from the heat.

10. When sufficiently cool to handle, using a small knife hollow out the pastries. Fill with the chicken mixture. Sprinkle with black pepper and minced parsley.

Creamy Hot Pastrami Filled Yorkies

Usually served with roast beef, these Yorkshire puddings make equally tasty canapés stuffed with a creamy hot pastrami filling.

Servings: 12

Total Time: 30mins

Ingredients:

- 12 store-bought frozen Yorkshire puddings
- 2 tbsp creamed, ready-made horseradish
- 2 tbsp wholegrain mustard
- 2 tbsp sour cream
- 12 slices pastrami
- 2 tbsp crispy onions

Directions:

1. Bake the Yorkshire puddings according to the package directions.

2. In the meantime, in a bowl, combine the horseradish with the mustard, and sour cream. Mix well to incorporate.

3. Fold a slice of pastrami and place into each of the puddings.

4. Top with a spoonful of creamy horseradish, garnish with crispy onions and serve.

Grilled Zucchini with Peanut Chicken

Grilled zucchini with a spicy, fragrant chicken topping make the perfect easy canapé.

Servings: 16

Total Time: 20mins

Ingredients:

- 2 medium-size zucchinis (diagonally cut into ½" slices)
- ⅛ tsp salt

- ⅛ tsp black pepper

Topping:

- ¼ cup water
- 3 tbsp brown sugar
- 2 tbsp soy sauce
- 1 tbsp smooth peanut butter
- 1 tsp fresh lime juice
- ¼ tsp ground ginger
- ¼ tsp cayenne pepper
- 1 cup cooked chicken (shredded)
- 2 tbsp red onion (peeled, and finely chopped
- Fresh cilantro (chopped, to garnish)

Directions:

1. Arrange the zucchini on a lightly oiled grill rack over moderate heat and while covered, grill for 3-4 minutes on each side, until tender. Season with salt and black pepper.

2. In a pan, whisk the water with the sugar, soy sauce, peanut butter, lime juice, ground ginger, and cayenne pepper. Bring to boil before reducing the heat to a simmer and cook uncovered and while occasionally stirring for 2-3 minutes, until slightly thickened.

3. Stir in the shredded chicken followed by the red onion and warm through.

4. When you are ready to serve, top the slices of zucchini with the chicken mixture and garnish with fresh cilantro.

Mini Lamb Kebabs with Yogurt Sauce

Get your party off to a great start with these tasty canapés.

Servings: 24

Total Time: 25mins

Ingredients:

- 17½ ounces minced lamb
- 1 tsp ground cumin
- 2 tsp ground coriander
- 3 cloves of garlic (peeled, and finely chopped, divided)

- 1 tbsp oil
- ½ small bunch of flat-leaf parsley (finely chopped)

Yogurt sauce:

- 7 ounces natural yogurt
- A few sprigs of fresh mint (chopped)
- 1 tbsp freshly squeezed lemon juice
- Special Equipment:
- Wooden skewers (soaked)

Directions:

1. In a bowl, combine the minced lamb with the cumin, coriander and ⅔ of the chopped garlic.

2. Evenly divide the mixture into 24 balls.

3. Push the balls onto the mini skewers and transfer to the fridge, to chill.

4. In the meantime, in a bowl, combine yogurt with the mint and fresh lemon juice: taste, and season.

5. Lightly brush the kebabs with oil and place under a moderate-high heat grill. Cook, while occasionally turning for 15 minutes, until cooked through.

6. When sufficiently cooked, roll the balls in the parsley and serve with the homemade yogurt sauce.

Mini Parma Ham Vegetable Tarts

Save time and calories by kicking the pastry into touch, and instead make these savory tarts featuring a Parma ham base.

Servings: 8

Total Time: 25mins

Ingredients:

- 2 medium-size eggs
- 6¾ ounces cream
- 5¼ ounces mixed veggies, of choice (chopped)
- 1 tbsp store-bought pesto

- 8 slices Parma ham

Directions:

1. Preheat the main oven to 395 degrees F.

2. In a jug combine the eggs with the cream, veggies, and pesto.

3. Use the Parma ham, to line 8-cups of a muffin tray.

4. Pour the egg-pesto on top of the ham.

5. Bake in the oven for between 15-20 minutes, until the egg is touch-set.

6. Set aside to cool before serving.

Moroccan Chickpea Patties

These chickpea patties are the best-ever finger food! Serve with hot harissa or a creamy sauce for dipping perfection.

Servings: 16

Total Time: 35mins

Ingredients:

- 1 onion (peeled, and sliced)
- 1 tbsp oil
- 2 cloves of garlic (peeled, and chopped)

- 1 (14½ ounce) can chickpeas (rinsed and drained)
- 2-3 spring onions (trimmed, and chopped)
- 4 tbsp fresh coriander (chopped)
- 4 tbsp breadcrumbs
- ½ tsp paprika
- ½ tsp ground cumin
- Salt and black pepper
- 2-3 tbsp polenta

Directions:

1. In a pan, fry the onion in oil until softened, for 5 minutes.

2. Add the garlic to the pan and fry for 60 seconds.

3. Transfer to a food processor and add the chickpeas along with the spring onions, coriander, breadcrumbs, paprika, cumin, a pinch of salt and a dash of pepper. Processor to a coarse paste.

4. Divide the mixture into 16 portions, and form into balls. Using the heel of your palm, flatten the balls to make patties.

5. Dip the patties in the polenta to evenly coat.

6. In batches, fry in a drop of oil for 2-3 minutes, on each side.

7. Serve with harissa or your favorite dip and enjoy.

Pecan-Stuffed Dates

Dates are perfect for stuffing so remove their pit and pack them full with a tasty filling. Serve, and enjoy.

Servings: 12

Total Time: 30mins

Ingredients:

- 2 tbsp olive oil
- 1 shallot (finely chopped)
- Salt
- 1 clove of garlic (peeled, and crushed)
- 1¾ ounces fresh breadcrumbs
- 3½ ounces pecans (finely chopped)
- 1 tbsp thyme leaves (chopped)
- ¼ cup vegetable stock
- 12 Medjool dates (pitted)
- 12 small-size sage leaves

Directions:

1. In a frying pan, heat the oil.

2. Add the shallot to the pan along with a pinch of salt and cook until softened, for 2-3 minutes.

3. Next, add the garlic followed by the breadcrumbs, pecans, and thyme and cook for an additional 60 seconds.

4. Add a splash of stock, to help bring the mixture together and put to one side.

5. Preheat the oven to 355 degrees F.

6. Slice the dates in half lengthways, taking care not to cut all the way through.

7. Stuff small balls of the garlic-thyme mixture into the dates and push the sides together.

8. Place a sage leaf on top of each date.

9. Arrange the stuffed dates on a parchment-lined baking tray.

10. Liberally brush the dates with olive oil and bake in the oven for between 15-20 minutes, until the sage is crisp.

11. Serve and enjoy.

Polenta and Prosciutto Chips

Pass on the potato chips, and instead prepare a batch of these utterly amazing polenta and prosciutto chips.

Servings: 20

Total Time: 20mins

Ingredients:

- 8¾ ounce ready-made block of polenta (cut into 20 chunky strips)

- 1 tbsp olive oil
- Freshly ground black pepper
- 3½ ounces prosciutto (sliced into 20 strips)
- 1 ounce Parmesan cheese

Directions:

1. Preheat the main oven to 395 degrees F.

2. Add the polenta to a bowl and combine with the oil and a few grounds of fresh black pepper, mix well to incorporate.

3. Wrap one prosciutto strip around a strip of polenta and place on a baking tray. Repeat the process until all 20 chips are assembled.

4. Scatter the Parmesan over all 20 chips.

5. Bake in the preheated oven until golden, this will take around 15 minutes.

6. Enjoy.

Ravioli Pops

Pop in the mouth cheese ravioli to dip in a warm Italian-style marinara sauce make for an incredibly moreish canape.

Servings: 40-45

Total Time: 35mins

Ingredients:

- ½ cup dry breadcrumbs
- 2 tsp pepper
- 1½ tsp dried oregano
- 1½ tsp dried parsley flakes

- 1 tsp salt
- 1 tsp crushed red pepper flakes
- ⅓ cup all-purpose flour
- 2 large-size eggs (lightly beaten)
- 1 (9 ounce) package refrigerated cheese ravioli
- Oil (to fry)
- Parmesan cheese (freshly grated)
- 40-45 popsicle sticks
- Marinara sauce (store-bought, warmed)

Directions:

1. In a shallow bowl, combine the breadcrumbs with the pepper, dried oregano, parsley flakes, salt, and red pepper.

2. To a second shallow bowl add the flour.

3. To a third shallow bowl, add the eggs.

4. Dip the ravioli first in the eggs, then the breadcrumbs. Shake off any excess before repeating the process. Gently pat to ensure the coating adheres to the pasta.

5. Heat ½" of oil in a skillet to a temperature of 395 degrees F.

6. In batches, fry the ravioli for 1-2 minutes on each side until golden. Using a slotted spoon, remove the fried ravioli from the oil and set aside on kitchen paper to drain. Keep warm.

7. Scatter grated Parmesan over the ravioli before inserting a popsicle stick into each one.

8. Serve with warmed marinara sauce, for dipping.

Salmon Mousse Canapés

The height of sophistication and elegance, these salmon mousse canapés are guaranteed to impress. For the wow factor, serve with a chilled Champagne cocktail.

Servings: 36

Total Time: 30mins

Ingredients:

- 2 English cucumbers
- 1 (8 ounce) package cream cheese (softened)

- ½ pound smoked salmon
- 1 tbsp 2% milk
- 1 tsp lemon-pepper seasoning
- 1 tsp fresh dill (snipped)
- Salt and black pepper (to taste)
- ½ cup heavy whipping cream
- Fresh dill (snipped, to serve)

Directions:

1. First create a decorative edge to the cucumbers, by peeling off strips and cutting each cucumber into ½" slices.

2. With a melon baller, remove some cucumber seeds from the center of each slice to create a well.

3. Add the cream cheese along with the salmon, milk, lemon pepper seasoning and dill to food blender or processor, cover and process to blend.

4. Transfer the mixture to a bowl and season with salt and black pepper.

5. In a second bowl, beat the cream until it can hold stiff peaks. Fold the cream into the cream cheese mixture.

6. Spoon the mousse onto the slices of cucumber, garnish with fresh dill and place in the fridge until you are ready to serve.

7. Serve chilled.

Spanish Skewers with Homemade Dip

Ole! Tuck into these tasty chorizo, potato, and pepper skewers and enjoy with a chilled homemade dip.

Servings: 24

Total Time: 50mins

Ingredients:

- 7 ounces waxy potatoes (peeled, and cut into ¾" chunks)

- 1 tbsp sunflower oil
- 2 tsp fresh rosemary (finely chopped)
- Salt and black pepper
- 1 large red pepper (seeded, cut into ¾" chunks)
- 1 large green pepper (seeded, cut into ¾" chunks)
- 7 ounces cooking chorizo (cut into 24 evenly-sized pieces)

Dip:

- 7 ounces reduced-fat crème fraiche
- 1 clove garlic (peeled, and crushed)
- ½ small pack flat-leaf parsley (finely chopped)

Special equipment:

- 24 short bamboo skewers

Directions:

1. Preheat the oven to 400 degrees F.

2. Bring a half-filled large pan of water to boil.

3. Add the potatoes to the pan and return to boil. Cook for 60 seconds, before draining and transferring to a bowl.

4. Pour the oil over the potatoes and scatter with rosemary. Season with salt and black pepper and toss to coat evenly.

5. Arrange the potatoes on a large baking tray and cook for 5 minutes. Flip the potatoes over and add the peppers. Cook for an additional 10 minutes, until they are beginning to soften. Set to one side to cool.

6. Thread the peppers along with a chunk of potato and a piece of chorizo onto the skewers. Arrange the skewers on a baking tray lined with parchment paper, cover and chill in the fridge for no more than 8 hours.

7. To prepare the dip: In a bowl, combine the crème fraiche with the garlic, and parsley. Cover and chill in the fridge, until needed.

8. When you are ready to serve, heat your oven to 400 degrees F.

9. Bake the skewers in the oven for 8-10 minutes, until the veggies are browned and the chorizo is cooked through.

10. Serve the skewers with the homemade dip.

Spicy Salmon and Guacamole Cones

This Mexican inspired canapé comes together in just half an hour. It's hot, it's spicy and it's easy to make – what's not to like?

Servings: 16

Total Time: 30mins

Ingredients:

Marinade:

- 1 red chili
- Zest of 1 fresh lime

- 3 scallions (coarsely chopped)
- Small bunch of fresh coriander (divided)
- 1 tomato
- 1 tsp superfine sugar

Salmon:

- 3 (4½ ounce) skinless salmon fillets
- 1 (11 ounce) bag of corn tortillas
- 7 ounces store-bought guacamole
- ½ cucumber (cut in half lengthways, seeded, and thinly sliced)
- Fresh lime wedges (to serve)

Directions:

1. In a food blender or processor, process the chili with the lime zest, scallions, half of the coriander, tomato and superfine sugar to a coarse consistency.

2. Arrange the salmon fillets on a baking tray.

3. Spoon the chili marinade over the fish and set aside for half an hour.

4. Heat the grill to high heat, and cook the salmon until cooked through, for 10-12 minutes. Flake the fish into lite chunks.

5. Warm the corn tortillas according to the package directions.

6. Slice the tortillas in half and roll each one into a cone. Use the center of each straight edge as a guide.

7. Add 1 tsp of guacamole to each cone followed by 2-3 slices of cucumber, coriander leaves and flaked salmon.

8. Serve with wedges of fresh lime and enjoy.

Steak on a Stick

This meaty canapé recipe is sure to be a firm favorite with steak lovers everywhere.

Servings: 8

Total Time: 12mins

Ingredients:

- 1 garlic clove (peeled, and crushed)
- 1 tbsp thyme leaves
- Grated zest of 1 lime

- 1 tsp Worcestershire sauce
- 2 tsp olive oil
- 14 ounces (1" thick) steak
- Freshly squeezed juice of 1 lime
- Wedges of lime (to serve)

Directions:

1. Combine the garlic, thyme, lime zest, Worcestershire sauce and olive oil in a small bowl.

2. Place the steak in a shallow baking dish and rub it all over with the garlic-lime mixture. Set aside to marinate for a couple of hours.

3. Squeeze the lime juice over the steak.

4. On high heat, in a hot griddle pan, sear the meat for a few minutes on each side. It is important not to overcook the steak, or it could become tough.

5. Transfer the steak to a plate and cover with aluminum foil. Set aside to rest for 10 minutes.

6. Cut the meat into cubes and spear with cocktail sticks.

7. Serve with wedges of fresh lime.

Stilton and Chutney Rarebit Nibbles

Elegant canapés can make or break a party or get-together, and these bites are super tasty.

Servings: 8

Total Time: 55mins

Ingredients:

Chutney:

- 2 red onions (peeled, and thinly sliced)
- 4 tbsp Muscovado sugar

- 3⅓ ounces balsamic vinegar

Rarebit:

- 10½ ounces stilton (crumbled)
- 7 ounces Parmesan cheese (freshly grated)
- 2 tbsp crème fraiche
- 2 medium-size eggs (beaten)
- 2 tsp wholegrain mustard
- Salt and black pepper
- 6 slices German rye bread

Directions:

1. Add the red onions along with the sugar and balsamic vinegar to a pan, and over low heat, cook while occasionally stirring for 25 minutes. The mixture should be sticky and gloopy. Set aside to cool.

2. In a bowl, combine the stilton with the Parmesan, crème fraiche, eggs, and wholegrain mustard. Taste and season and place in the fridge, to chill.

3. When you are ready to serve, heat the grill and lightly toast the rye bread. Cut the bread into chunks.

4. Arrange the bread on a baking sheet.

5. Spread 1 tsp of chutney over each chunk before piling on the cheese mixture.

6. Grill until bubbling and browned, for 3-5 minutes.

Sweet Corn Beignets with Spicy Salsa

Serve these crisp, sweet corn beignets alongside your next party spread.

Servings: 15-20

Total Time: 25mins

Ingredients:

- Sunflower oil (to fry)

Salsa:

- 2 medium-size zucchinis (finely diced)
- 1 green chili (diced)
- 1 clove of garlic (peeled, and grated)
- 1 green tomato (diced)
- 1 tsp coriander (chopped)
- Freshly squeezed juice of 1 lime
- Salt and black pepper

Beignets:

- 3 sweet corn cobs (cooked, kernels removed)
- 7 ounces tapioca flour
- 5¼ ounces polenta
- ½ tsp bicarbonate of soda
- ¼ tsp garlic powder
- ¼ tsp chili flakes
- 1 tsp cumin seeds (toasted)
- 1½ cups cider
- Flaky sea salt
- 1 tbsp rapeseed oil

Directions:

1. To prepare the salsa: In a frying pan, heat the oil over moderate-high heat.

2. Fry the zucchini in the oil for a few minutes, until lightly colored.

3. Remove the zucchini from the pan and while still hot, combine with the chili, garlic, tomato, and coriander. Set aside to cool, before seasoning with fresh lime juice, salt, and pepper. Set to one side.

4. In a food blender, or processor, puree $\frac{1}{3}$ of the corn kernels. Transfer the puree to a bowl, and combine with the tapioca followed by the polenta, bicarbonate of soda, garlic powder, chili flakes, and cumin seeds. Taste and season.

5. Whisk the cider into the mixture, add the remaining sweet corn and stir to create a batter.

6. Heat a deep-fat fryer to 355 degrees F.

7. In batches, deep-fry large spoonfuls of the batter until golden, for 1-2 minutes.

8. Using a slotted spoon, remove from the hot oil and place on a kitchen paper towel.

9. Garnish with flaky sea salt and serve with the homemade salsa.

Sweet

Apple Pie Pastry Wedges

These bite-size apple pastry wedges taste just as good as grandma's homemade apple pie.

Servings: 16

Total Time: 35mins

Ingredients:

- ½ cup sugar
- 2 tsp ground cinnamon
- 1 (14 ounce) package refrigerated pastry
- 3 tbsp butter (melted, and divided)

- 2 medium-size sharp green apples (each apple cut into 8 wedges)

Directions:

1. Preheat the main oven to 425 degrees F.

2. In a bowl, combine the sugar with the cinnamon. Set 1 tbsp of the mixture to one side.

3. On a lightly floured, worktop, roll out the pastry. Roll and trim each one to form an 8" square.

4. Brush the pastry with 2 tbsp of melted butter.

5. Sprinkle the remaining sugar mixture over the butter and cut each square into 8 (1") strips.

6. Wrap 1 strip of pastry around each apple wedges and place the sugary side of the pastry touching the fruit.

7. Arrange the slices on a parchment-lined baking sheet, brush the tops with the remaining melted butter and bake in the oven for 12-15 minutes, until browned.

8. Serve and enjoy warm.

Baby Caramel Rolls

It will take a lot longer to make these mini rolls that it will to finish them off! So maybe think about doubling up and making a bigger batch!

Servings: 12

Total Time: 35mins

Ingredients:

- ⅓ cup brown sugar
- ⅓ cup salted butter (chopped)
- 2 tbsp light corn syrup
- 1-½ tsp 2% milk

- 1 (8 ounce) tube refrigerated crescent rolls
- 2 tsp sugar
- ½ tsp ground cinnamon

Directions:

1. Preheat the main oven to 375 degrees F.

2. In a pan, combine the brown sugar with the butter, corn syrup, and milk. Cook while stirring over moderate heat until incorporated Transfer to a 9" greased pie plate.

3. Separate the dough into 4 rectangles, gently pressing perforations to seal.

4. In a bowl, mix the sugar with the ground cinnamon, and sprinkle the mixture evenly over the rectangles. Jelly roll style, roll up, beginning with the longest side, and pinching seams to seal.

5. Cut each roll into 9 even slices and cut side facing down place in the pie plate.

6. Bake in the preheated oven for 15-18 minutes until golden. Allow to cool for 60 seconds, before inverting onto a plate.

7. Serve and enjoy.

Caramel Cream Chocolate and Hazelnut Popsicles

Catering for a summer event? Then these frozen fancies are the answer!

Servings: 12

Total Time: 5hours 40mins

Ingredients:

- 2½ ounce chocolate hazelnut spread
- 3¾ ounces salted caramel cream
- Special Equipment:

- Popsicle sticks
- 12 small-size circular silicon molds

Directions:

1. First, melt the chocolate hazelnut spread in a bowl over a saucepan of simmering water. Set half of the mixture to one side.

2. Pour a thin layer of the chocolate hazelnut spread into the bottom of the 12 molds. Transfer to the fridge for half an hour.

3. Place a nut-size piece of salted caramel cream into each mold and cover with the half portion of chocolate hazelnut spread, set aside earlier.

4. Put a popsicle stick into each lolly and transfer to the freezer for 5-6 hours.

5. To release the popsicle, twist the molds and serve.

Key Lime Pie Shots

Dessert in a glass; the perfect sweet party canapé!

Servings: 20

Total Time: 15mins

Ingredients:

- 4 ounces reduced-fat cream cheese

- 14 ounces sweetened condensed milk
- Freshly squeezed juice of 3 fresh limes
- Zest of 3 fresh limes (divided)
- 15 graham cracker (crumbed)
- Whipped cream (to top)
- Wedges of lime (to serve)

Directions:

1. Using an electric or stand mixer, combine the cream cheese with the condensed milk.

2. Add the lime juice along with half of the lime zest and mix well to combine.

3. Transfer to a bowl, and place in the fridge for 2-8 hours.

4. To shooter glasses, add the cream cheese mixture followed by the graham crackers in alternating layers until full.

5. Add the whipped cream and lime zest.

6. Garnish with a wedge of lime and serve immediately.

Lemon Meringue Pots

Sharp and tangy, this citrus dessert served in a handy shot glass makes an ideal sweet treat.

Servings: 12

Total Time: 1hour 25mins

Ingredients:

- 2 gelatin leaves
- 7 ounces lemon curd
- 3½ ounces shortbread biscuits

- 5 ounces double cream
- 2 tbsp icing sugar
- 1 tsp vanilla essence
- 2 meringue nests
- Sprinkles (to decorate, optional)

Directions:

1. First, in cold water, soften the gelatin, for 5 minutes.

2. In a pan, over moderate heat, heat the lemon curd.

3. Remove the gelatin from the water, and carefully squeeze out any excess liquid. Stir into the hot lemon curd to entirely dissolve. Set to one side to slightly cool.

4. Spoon the mixture into 12 (2¾ ounce) shot glasses. Chill in the fridge for a minimum of 60 minutes.

5. In a food processor, process the shortbread biscuits to a rough crumb consistency.

6. Spoon approximately 1 tablespoon of the crumbs into each shot glass.

7. In a bowl, whip the cream, icing sugar and vanilla essence into soft peaks.

8. Pipe the cream mixture on top of the crumbs.

9. Crush the meringue and scatter it over the cream.

10. Decorate with sprinkles and enjoy.

Mini Orange Cupcakes

Mini cupcakes are great for parties, and these mini cupcakes are a real game-changer.

Servings: 48

Total Time: 50mins

Ingredients:

- ½ cup butter (softened)
- 1 cup sugar
- 2 large-size eggs
- 1 tbsp grated orange zest
- 1 tbsp freshly squeezed orange juice

- ½ tsp vanilla essence
- 1½ cups all-purpose flour
- 1½ tsp baking powder
- ¼ tsp salt
- ½ cup buttermilk

Buttercream:

- ½ cup butter (softened)
- ¼ tsp salt
- 2 cups powdered sugar
- 2 tbsp 2% milk
- 1½ tsp vanilla essence
- ½ cup orange marmalade

Directions:

1. Preheat the main oven to 325 degrees. Line 4 (12-mini muffin cups with paper liners).

2. In a bowl for the marmalade, cream the butter with the sugar, until fluffy and light.

3. One at a time, add the eggs, beat well after egg addition.

4. Beat in the zest along with the fresh orange juice and vanilla essence.

5. In a second bowl, whisk the flour with the baking powder and salt. Add to the creamed mixture alternating with the buttermilk and beat well after each addition.

6. Fill the prepared muffin cups to ⅔ full.

7. Bake in the oven for 10-12 minutes, until springy to the touch.

8. Set aside while still in the pans to cool before removing to wire baking racks to completely cool.

9. To prepare the buttercream: In a bowl, beat the butter with the salt until creamy.

10. Gradually beat in the powdered sugar, milk and vanilla essence until silky smooth.

11. With a paring knife, cut a 1" wide cone shape piece from the surface of each cake. Discard the removed piece and fill the space with the marmalade.

12. Spread or pipe the buttercream over the tops and enjoy.

Mini Pastel Macarons

You won't be able to resist these cute and colorful mini macarons.

Servings: 34

Total Time: 40mins

Ingredients:

- 5½ ounces ground almonds
- 9 ounces icing sugar (sifted)
- Seeds from 2 split vanilla pods
- 2 large-size egg whites

Coloring:

- Pastel pink, blue and yellow food coloring

Butter Cream:

- 5 ounces butter (softened)
- 10 ounces icing sugar (sifted, and divided)
- 1-2 tbsp milk (divided)
- 2 drops vanilla essence

Directions:

1. Preheat the main oven to 300 degrees F. Line several baking trays with parchment paper.

2. Add the ground almonds along with the icing sugar and vanilla seeds into a bowl.

3. In a second bowl, whisk the egg whites until firm and fold them into the almond mixture.

4. Divide the mixture into three, and add the pink coloring to one portion, the blue to the second portion and the yellow to the third. You will only need 1-2 drops of each.

5. Spoon the mixture into an icing bag and pipe small mounds approximately 1" in diameter onto the prepared trays. Space the mounds well apart from each other. Allow to stand for 2 minutes, so that the tops dry.

6. Transfer to the preheated oven and bake for 20-25 minutes before cooling on a wire baking rack.

7. In a bowl, beat the butter until softened.

8. Add 5 ounces of the sifted icing sugar along with 1 tablespoon of milk and the vanilla essence, beating until creamy.

9. Add additional icing sugar to thicken or a drop more milk to thin, if necessary.

10. Sandwich the macarons together with a small amount of vanilla buttercream.

Shortcakelettes

Not only are these mini strawberry shortcakes delicious, but they're also totally adorable too!

Servings: N/A*

Total Time: 40mins

Ingredients:

- 1 readymade pound cakes
- 1 cup whipped cream
- 4 ounces full-fat cream cheese
- 2 tbsp granulated sugar
- Fresh strawberries (sliced)**

Directions:

1. Cut the prepared pound cake into ½" slices. Using a small, circular cookie cutter, cut small rounds out of the cake slices.

2. Fold together the whipped cream and cream cheese until combined. Taste and sweeten with granulated sugar if necessary.

3. Top each cake round with a generous spoonful of the cream mixture and garnish with ¾ strawberry slices. Serve.

*Dependent on the size of cookie cutter used.

**You will need enough whole strawberries to top each shortcake portion with 3-4 strawberry slices.

Strawberry Cheesecake Pots

This sweet treat is proof positive that canapés needn't only be savory!

Servings: 6

Total Time: 45mins

Ingredients:

- 2½ ounces light digestive biscuits
- 7 ounces light condensed milk
- Zest of 1 lemon
- Freshly squeezed juice of 1 lemon
- 1 tsp vanilla essence

- 5¼ ounces extra-light cream cheese
- 5¼ ounces no-fat Greek yogurt
- 8¾ ounces fresh strawberries (washed, hulled and chopped)
- 3 tbsp strawberry jam

Directions:

1. Crumble the biscuits into a bowl, and evenly divide the crumbs between 6 small tumblers or wine glasses.

2. Pour the milk into a second bowl and add the lemon zest along with the juice and vanilla essence, stir well until thickened.

3. Whisk the cream cheese along with the Greek yogurt in a bowl, until silky smooth. Fold the mixture into the milk mixture, taking care not to over-beat.

4. Spoon the mixture over the crumbs and chill in the fridge for 30-60 minutes.

5. Mix the strawberries with the jam and spoon over the individual cheesecakes.

6. Serve.

Sweet Potato Cheesecakes

No canapé collection would be complete without these no-bake cheesecakes.

Servings: 8

Total Time: 4hours 25mins

Ingredients:

- 4 tbsp unsalted butter (melted)
- ⅔ cup graham cracker crumbs
- 8 ounces cream cheese (room temperature)
- 6 ounces mascarpone cheese (room temperature)

- 2/3 cup sweet potato puree
- ¾ cup sweetened condensed milk
- 1 tsp vanilla essence
- ¼ tsp salt
- ¼ tsp cinnamon
- Whipped cream (to top)
- Cinnamon (to serve)
- Graham crumbs (to serve)

Directions:

1. In a bowl, combine the butter with the graham crumbs until moist.

2. Press the crumbs into ramekins using the back of a spoon.

3. Using an electric mixer, beat the cream cheese with the mascarpone cheese until smooth and combine. You will need to scrape down the side of the bowl as necessary.

4. Add the sweet potato puree and mix until smooth.

5. On low speed, and using the mixer, gradually drizzle in the milk, while still scraping down the sides until the mixture is silky smooth.

6. Add the vanilla essence, along with the salt and cinnamon and beat well to combine.

7. Spoon the mixture over the top of the crumbs in the ramekins and place in the fridge for 4-6 hours.

8. Top with whipped cream, a sprinkle of cinnamon and a scattering of crumbs.

9. Serve.

Cocktails

Blood Orange and Lemon Prosecco Slushies

A grown-up take on a childhood classic drink. Bubbly Prosecco is poured over zesty lemon and blood orange sorbet for a refreshing, fruity tipple.

Servings: 8

Total Time: 5mins

Ingredients:

- Angostura bitters
- 2 pints blood orange sorbet

- 2 pints lemon sorbet
- 2 bottles Prosecco (chilled)
- Fresh mint

Directions:

1. To the bottom of 8 glasses, add a few dashes of Angostura bitters.

2. Add a scoop each of blood orange and lemon sorbet to each glass.

3. Top each glass up with chilled Prosecco.

4. Garnish with fresh mint and serve straight away.

Blueberry Lavender Fizz

This cocktail is a party must-have. It's light, refreshing, and fruitylicious!

Servings: 8

Total Time: 25mins

Ingredients:

- Blueberries (for ice cubes)

- 1 cup blueberries
- 1 cup lavender sugar
- 1 cup water
- 1 ounce good-quality vodka
- Freshly squeezed juice from 1 lime
- Soda water

Directions:

1. Place a blueberry or two in 8 ice cube molds and fill with water. Freeze.

2. In a pan, combine 1 cup of blueberries with the lavender sugar, and water. Bring to boil, stirring to dissolve the sugar entirely. Turn the heat down and simmer for 10 minutes, until the mixture starts to thicken slightly.

3. Strain the mixture through a mesh sieve, gently pressing down on the berries to extract as much juice as is possible.

4. Fill each of the 8 glasses with the berry ice cubes, 1 tbsp of blueberry syrup along with 1 ounce of vodka and top with lime juice.

5. Top with club soda and serve.

Brandy and Pineapple Party Punch

Sweet tasting with a warm hint of nutmeg, this party punch is the quintessential drink to serve with savory canapés.

Servings: 8

Total Time: 45mins

Ingredients:

- 12 ounces brandy
- 6 ounces fresh pineapple juice
- 3 ounces fresh lime juice

- 3 ounces simple syrup*
- Pinch of freshly grated nutmeg
- 9 ounces club soda (chilled)
- Ice
- Lemon wheels (to garnish)

Directions:

1. In a large jug or pitcher, combine the brandy with the pineapple juice and lime juice. Add the simple syrup and nutmeg, and transfer to the fridge to chill for half an hour.

2. Pour in the club soda and stir to combine.

3. Serve over lots of ice and garnish with a lemon wheel.

*For the simple syrup: Combine equal parts of water and sugar in a pan. Bring to a boil, while constantly stirring to dissolve the sugar entirely. Allow to cool and use as needed.

Perfect Pimms

This quintessential British summertime beverage has a history spanning almost two centuries. Cheers!

Servings: 4

Total Time: 1hour 30mins

Ingredients:

- 1¼ cups gin
- 1¼ cups red vermouth
- ¾ cup orange liqueur

- 1 medium-size orange (halved, seeded and sliced)
- 1 medium-size lemon (halved, seeded and sliced)
- 1 cucumber (sliced)
- Tonic water (chilled)
- Sprigs of mint (to garnish)

Directions:

1. Around 2-3 hours before serving, in a large pitcher, combine the gin with the red vermouth and orange liqueur, and stir well to combine.

2. Add 4 slices each of orange and lemon along with 8 slices of cucumber. Cover the pitcher and place in the fridge to chill.

3. To serve, top with the chilled tonic water and serve in tall glasses over ice.

4. Garnish with the remaining slices of orange and lemon and a mint sprig.

Pink Lemonade

This pretty pink lemonade may seem innocent, but with a whole bottle of rose wine inside it's definitely party-perfect!

Servings: 8-10

Total Time: 30mins

Ingredients:

- 12 ounces frozen pink lemonade concentrate (thawed)
- 1 quart club soda
- 1 bottle rosé wine
- Lemon slices

Directions:

1. In a large pitcher, combine the thawed pink lemonade concentrate, club soda, and rosé wine.

2. Fill the pitcher with ice and lemon slices, allow to chill for half an hour before dividing between ice-filled glasses and serving.

Pomegranate Bellini

Tart yet sweet pomegranate juice combines with chilled Prosecco to create the perfect Bellini.

Servings: 4

Total Time: 3mins

Ingredients:

- 6 ounces pomegranate juice (chilled)
- 1 bottle of Prosecco (chilled)

- Pomegranate arils (to garnish)
- Lime twist (to garnish)

Directions:

1. Pour 1 ounce of pomegranate juice into 6 Champagne flutes.

2. Top each one with Prosecco.

3. Garnish with pomegranate arils and finish with a lime twist.

Sgroppino

The perfect cocktail to serve with sweet canapés. Sgroppino loosely translates as little un-knotter, meaning it helps to cut through all the overindulgence!

Servings: 6

Total Time:

Ingredients:

- 12 scoops store-bought lemon sorbet
- 5 ounces vodka

- 5 ounces Prosecco (chilled)
- Lemon rind (to garnish)

Directions:

1. Add the lemon sorbet to a large punch bowl.

2. Pour the vodka and Prosecco over the sorbet and whisk to a silky smooth consistency.

3. Pour into chilled Champagne flutes.

4. Garnish with lemon rind and serve.

Sparkling Royal Punch

Elegant canapés deserve to be served alongside an aristocratic drink, and this punch is fit for a king and queen.

Servings: 12-15

Total Time: 5mins

Ingredients

- ½ cup sugar
- 1 bottle red burgundy
- 4 ounces brandy
- 2 bottles brut champagne
- 4 cups sparkling water
- Fresh strawberries (hulled, halved)

- 2 oranges (peeled, seeded, sliced into thin wheels)

Directions:

1. In a punch bowl, dissolve the sugar in the burgundy.

2. Pour in the brandy followed by the champagne and water.

3. Add a block of ice to the bowl.

4. Decorate with strawberries and slices of orange.

5. Serve and enjoy.

Strawberry and Watermelon Mojitos

This cocktail pairs perfectly with either cheese or prosciutto so be sure to include it at your next get-together with friends.

Servings: 8

Total Time: 25mins

Ingredients:

- 4 pounds watermelon (rind removed, seeded, and cut in half)
- ½ cup strawberry flavor liqueur
- 1 cup white rum
- 5 fresh limes (cut into wedges, and seeded)
- 3 cups lemonade (chilled)
- 2 cups of ice
- Mint sprigs (to garnish)

Directions:

1. Using a spoon or melon-baller, scoop one half of the watermelon into balls and place in a bowl.

2. Coarsely chop the remaining half of watermelon.

3. Add the chopped watermelon to a blender and process until smooth. Strain the mixture into a large pitcher or jug.

4. Pour in the liqueur along with the white rum.

5. Squeeze the juice from the wedges of lime into the watermelon mixture and add the wedges of lime.

6. Pour in the lemonade followed by the watermelon balls and 2 cups of ice.

7. Garnish with sprigs of mint and enjoy.

The Bee's Knees

Simply the best, this gin cocktail is the perfect complement to all number of canapés.

Servings: 1*

Total Time: 6mins

Ingredients:

- Honey Syrup:
- 1 cup honey
- 1 cup hot water

Cocktail:

- 1 ounces freshly squeezed lemon juice
- ¾ ounce honey syrup (see recipe)
- 2 ounces good-quality gin
- Ice

Directions:

1. For the syrup: In a large container, combine the honey with the hot water, stirring until entirely incorporated.

2. In a cocktail shaker, combine the fresh lemon juice with the honey syrup, gin, and ice.

3. Shake and strain into a coupe glass.

*Adjust the quantities to allow for your number of guests.

Printed in Great Britain
by Amazon